Houston

A Photographic Tour of my Hometown

Houston

A Photographic Tour of my Hometown

AVA RODRIGUEZ

Assisted by
PERCY CABOT

ARCHER TRENT, PUBLISHER
2017

COPYRIGHT © 2017 THE GRIFFOUN SOCIETY & AVA RIDGIGUEZ

ALL RIGHTS RESERVED.

Neither this book nor any portion thereof may be reproduced or used in any manner whatsoever without the express written permission of the copyright owners, except, of course, as specified in the fair-use clause.

First Printing: 2017

A Fine-Art Project of the
GRIFFOUN SOCIETY

ISBN 978-0-9990029-1-9

For my mother,
Gina Bocanegra

CONTENTS

INTRODUCTION

Section I
DOWNTOWN DISTRICT
Pages 1 through 34

Section II
NORTH SIDE AND EAST END
Pages 35 through 44

Section III
MID-TOWN & MUSEUM DISTRICT
Pages 45 through 54

Section IV
MONTROSE DISTRICT & WESTHEIMER
Pages 55 through 58

Section V
THE HEIGHTS
Pages 59 through 64

Section VI
FESTIVALS & STREET FAIRS
Pages 65 through 94

NOTES

INTRODUCTION

I love Houston. I was born here. I have spent my entire life here, but that does not mean that I have not traveled. I have seen other cities, and Houston shines by comparison to most.

So let me take you on a little tour. I want to show you some of the things about my hometown that I like best. Of course, I cannot in a single volume include everything that I might wish to, just as I could not in a single day take you by car or by bus to all the places I think you should see. My plan, therefore, is to focus on the heart of Houston: the Downtown District and some of the inner-loop neighborhoods. To my thinking, these, the oldest parts of town with the longest histories, are the most fascinating. But that means that I shall be neglecting NASA and Clear Lake, the Texas Medical Center, the Port of Houston, Sugar Land, La Porte, Pasadena, Pearland, Missouri City, Spring, and many other communities in the Greater Houston area, any one of which might provide enchanting images enough to fill a book like this one.

Incidentally, I have divided this project into six sections, the first five being defined by the geographic areas they cover and the last devoted to festivals and street fairs.

Houstonians love to party. Our galas are epic and represent every world culture. Nor are the festivities confined to the ethnic communities in which they originated. On St Patrick's Day, for instance, everyone is Irish. On the Buddhist New Year, we are all Asian. And on Cinco de Mayo, a non-Mexican is not to be found. Every weekend we flock to crafts fairs and flea markets. We love to get together in huge numbers. We look for any excuse to stage a parade.

Houston with a population of 2,239,558 is the fourth largest city in the United States; and yet, quite remarkably, there prevails here a sense of community, such as one would expect to find only in a village or hamlet. It is the quality I like best about my hometown. I sometimes tell people that I grew up in the biggest small town in America. I hope the city portrait that we have created here communicates that particular characteristic. ❖

I
Downtown District

Main Street Square

Public Sculpture

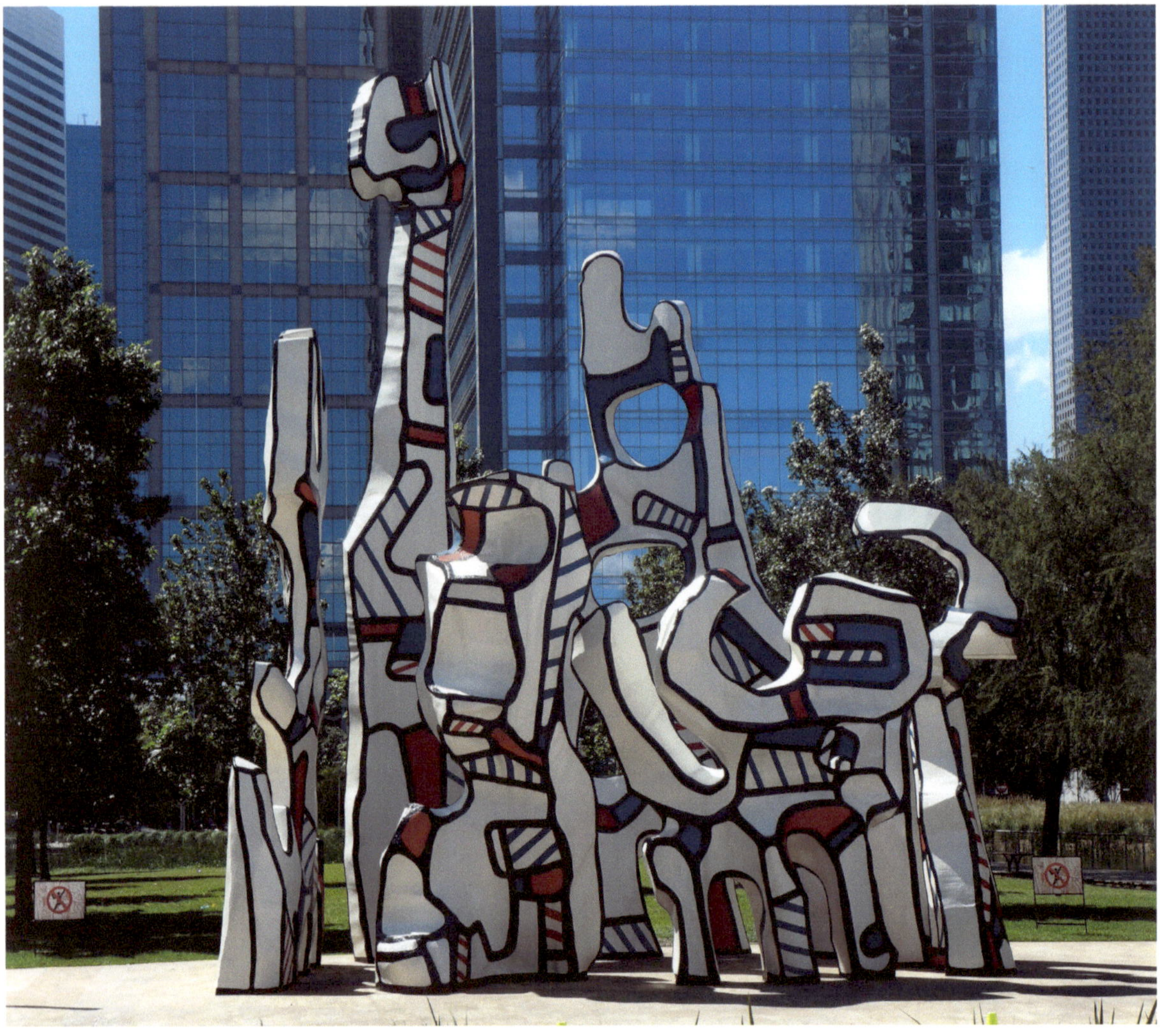

MONUMENT AU FANTOME
BY JEAN DUBUFFET
A GIFT FROM THE DUNCAN FAMILY

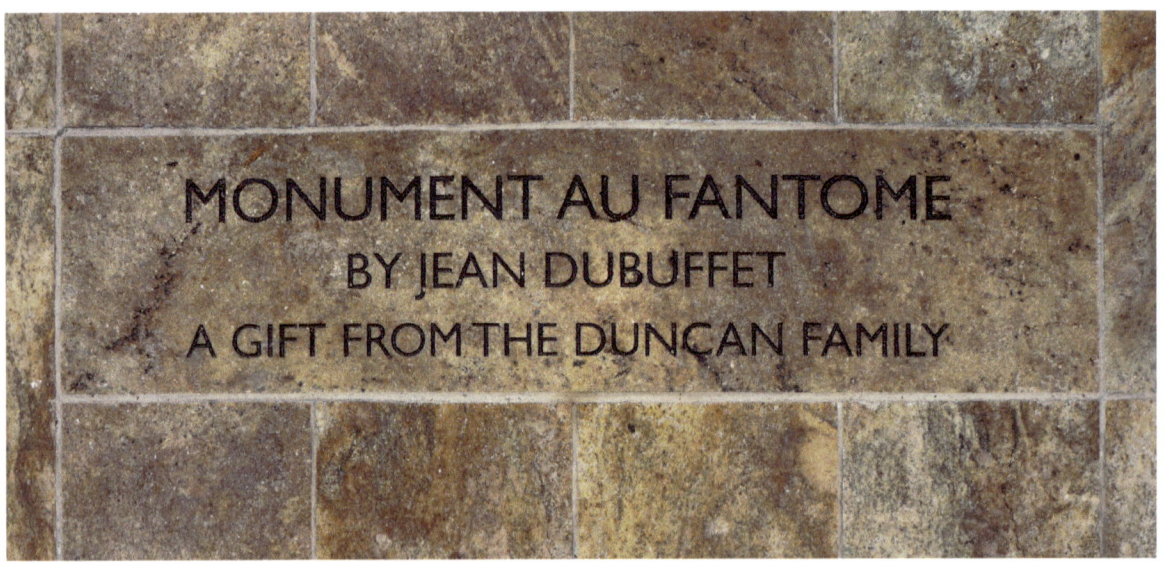

Annunciation Church (above)　　　Christ Church Cathedral (below)

Harris County Criminal Courthouse

George H W Bush Monument

Capital Fragment from Old City Hall 1904-1960

This old sign, still visible in the 400 block of Main Street, dates back to 1923.

Allen's Landing on Buffalo Bayou is where, during the nineteenth century, barges loaded and unloaded cargoes of cotton, pelts, coffee, sugar, salt, saddles, rice, lumber, and other goods.

Club Quarters

Lancaster Hotel

The old Chase Building (not to be confused with the newer Chase Tower, which is the tallest building on the Houston skyline) is one of the finest examples of Art Deco architecture to be seen anywhere. It is very probably the most photographed building in Houston. Art students and architecture students alike take field trips here to sketch the structure's elaborate ornamentation.

1001 Fannin Street

Heritage Society
Sam Houston Park

Root Memorial Square

31

Avenida de las Americas (above) Discovery Green (below)

Discovery Green

Seto and Noyola

II
North Side
& East End

Canal Street

III
Mid-town & Museum District

Pensive

Metro Light Rail

50

Descending Night by Adolph Alexander Weinman
Museum of Fine Arts, Houston

IV
Montrose District & Westheimer

V
The Heights

VI
FESTIVALS
& STREET FAIRS

Dragon-Boat Races

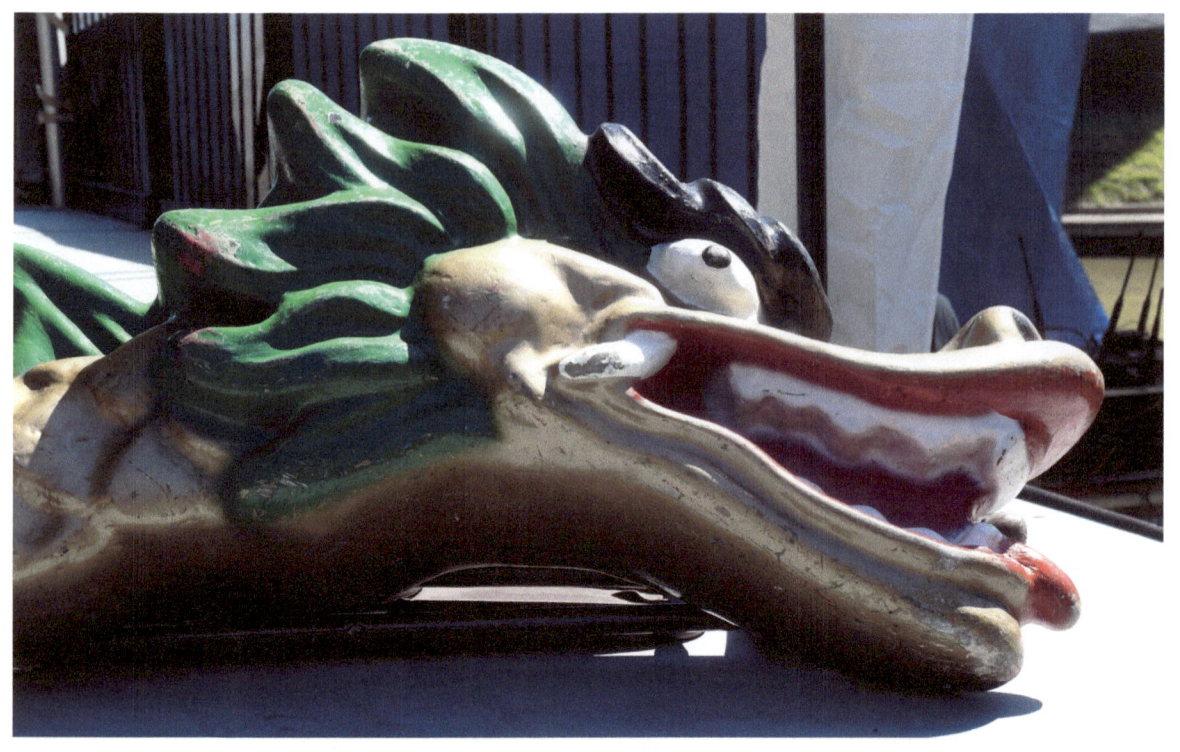

Philippine Folk Dancers

Pride Day

Art-Car Events

Food Trucks

First a selfie; then the food trucks.

COMICPALOOZA

Anime Convention

Liz Coleman is taking a break from watching a parade that seems to have gone on forever.

Bazaars & Flea Markets

Celebrating the Year of the Rooster

NOTES

Page 4: Sculpture by Floyd Newsum

Page 5: Sculpture by Joan Miró

Page 7: This blacksmith sculpture stands on the grounds of Minute Maid Park. What its relationship is to baseball or to Union Station, which once occupied this space, no one has been able to tell me. Nor is there any plaque to identify the artist; however, the anvil bears the logo of the Stewart & Stevenson Company.

Page 8: This statue of Craig Biggio is by Robert Hogan, who also created a companion piece of Jeff Bagwell catching the ball thrown by Biggio to complete a spectacular double play.

Page 10 (bottom): Photo by Xiomara Roma (in collaboration with Percy Cabot and Parivash Jamshidi)

Page 11: Here I am at UHD (University of Houston, Downtown), where I am currently attending a three-week intensive summer transition program, having just graduated from hign school.

Page 12: The Sweeney, Coombs & Fredericks Building, designed by architect George E Dickey, was built in 1889 on the site of the 1861 Van Anstyne Building, some parts of which were saved and incorporated into the new Victorian structure.

Pages 13 and 14: Houston has more fountains and water features than any other city I've ever been in.

Page 15 (bottom): The Franklin Lofts represent a conversion from the old First National Bank Building.

Page 17: The Friedman Clock Tower features a Seth Thomas Clock from Houston's 1904 City Hall, which stood in Market Square.

Page 20: Market Square

Page 22 (bottom): The elegant old Rice Hotel has now been converted to loft apartments. This is the lobby.

Page 27 (bottom): Heritage Plaza, the same tall building that appears on the front cover

Page 28: The sign in the foreground identifies a building not in the picture. This is actually Wells Fargo Plaza.

Page 30: 1414 Austin Street

Page 31 (bottom): Root Memorial Square was donated to the City of Houston in 1923 by the family of Alexander Porter Root and Laura Shepherd Root in their memory. The sculpture group "Heritage Lanterns" by Carter Ernst and Paul Kittelson was added in 2005.

Page 32 (top): Pappadeaux Seafood Kitchens inside the George R Brown Convention Center is a great place to dine whenever you're visiting Avenida de las Americas.

Page 32 (bottom): Water Tree Fountain on Discovery Green

Pages 35 and 36 (bottom): All over town, traffic-signal switching boxes are being decorated by local artists. Those in the North Side celebrate Hispanic culture.

Page 36 (top): From Barnett Transit Center, you can get a really good view of the Downtown skyline. The tallest building is the Chase Tower.

Page 39: Our Lady of Guadalupe Catholic Church on Navigation Boulevard is where my grandparents were married in June of 1955. It is just down the street from the East End Market, where my mom and I sell Mexican candy with the La Colmena label established decades ago by my grandfather.

Page 40 (bottom): Mural detail, Talento Bilingüe de Houston

Page 41: The neighborhood immediately east of downtown is called EADO (for East Downtown).

Page 42 (top): EADO once aspired to be Houston's Chinatown, but today most of the Asian-owned business have moved elsewhere.

Pages 42 (bottom) and 43 (bottom): These colorful tiles decorate a retaining wall on Lockwood Drive near Telephone Road.

Page 43 (top): I'll bet nobody ever bothers Christine when she takes her dogs out for a walk. BBVA Compass Stadium (in the background) is home to the Houston Dash (women's soccer club) and the Houston Dynamo (men's soccer club).

Page 46: Here I am at Hermann Park trying to get a good picture of the famous Sam Houston equestrian statue by Enrico Cerracchio.

Page 47 (top): Photo by Parivash Jamshidi (used with her permission)

Pages 50 and 51: Lillie and Hugh Roy Cullen Sculpture Garden at MFAH features works by Auguste Rodin, Louise Bourgeois, Ellsworth Kelly, Henri Matisse, Joan Miró, and Pablo Picasso.

Page 53: This portrait bust by Jean-Antoine Houdon of John Paul Jones is in the permanent collection of the Museum of Fine Arts, Houston.

Page 54 (bottom): The Hotel Zaza (in the background) was formerly known as the Warwick Hotel.

Page 55: Bacchus Mediterranean Wine Bar and Coffee Shop

Page 56 (top): From Waugh Street looking east toward Downtown

Page 56 (bottom): Niko Niko's Greek and American Café

Page 57 (top): Colombe d' Or

Page 58 (bottom): Chinese Consulate

Page 68 (bottom): This photographer's name is *Cynthia*.

Page 73 (top): Filipino Young Professionals

Page 86 (bottom): Ingrid Pinzon, Claudia Lievano, and Holly Sullivan

Page 91 (top): Musae Imports at Waugh Flea

Page 91 (bottom): Vladimir Alexander does quickie portrait sketches every Sunday on the Navigation Esplanade.

Page 92: Second Saturday Montrose Arts Market

Page 93 (top): Artist Tracy Hamblin, East End Street Market

Page 93 (bottom): Fine Art Farms offers fresh produce at the East End Street Market every Sunday from 10:00 am until 2:00 pm.

Page 94 (top): Here I am with my mom at the East End Street Market, where we have our business, La Colmena Mexican Candy, set up in a pop-up tent. We take pride in bringing back to Houston our pralines and dulce de leche made from family recipes more than a hundred years old.

Page 94 (bottom): Credence is the daughter of Tracy Hamblin (top of page 93).

Page 95: Arunkon Vass, Simple Nut Organics, hand-crafted skin-care products

Page 96: Chinese New Year at the Museum of Fine Arts, Houston

OTHER LITERARY AND FINE-ART PROJECTS OF THE GRIFFOUN SOCIETY

Street Photography and Pencil Portraits (ISBN 978-1-365-51529-3) by Percy Cabot, 70 pages, fully illustrated in color on coated stock, 8.5" x 11" perfect-bound trade paperback

The Trudy Silverheels Scrapbook (ISBN 978-1-365-74226-2) edited by Xiomara Roma, 84 pages, fully illustrated in color on coated stock, 8.5" x 8.5" perfect-bound trade paperback, highly erotic (not for underage readers)

Dusky Nightshade and the Little Heathens (ISBN 978-0-9990029-0-2), novel by Trudy Silverheels, 228 pages, illustrated by Percy Cabot, 6" x 9" perfect-bound trade paperback

The Chosen Profession of Jade Stonecalf (ISBN 978-147-925046-2), novella by Trudy Silverheels, 106 pages, illustrated by Percy Cabot, 6" x 9" perfect-bound trade paperback

The Adventures of Pinky Valentine and Friends (ISBN 978-15404-5701-1), juvenile (pre-teen) fiction by Phoebe Synn and Trudy Silverheels, 136 pages, 5" x 8" perfect-bound trade paperback

Observations and Comtemplations of a Humanist (ISBN 978-0-692-85786-1), wisdom and inspiration by Leo Madrigal, 84 pages, 6" x 9" hardcover with dust jacket

Trudy Silverheels: Daybook of a Warrior Girl (ISBN 978-1542385312), memoir by Linda Yazzie (birth name of Trudy Silverheels), 144 pages, illustrated, 6" x 9" perfect-bound trade paperback

www.ingramcontent.com/pod-product-compliance
Lightning Source LLC
Chambersburg PA
CBHW041152290426
44108CB00002B/47